Oceanica

TRICIA D. WAGNER

LYRIDAE BOOKS

"Take an oar,"
said the waves,
candlelit by the stars.
"Bold adventures are waiting for you."

One

How fine the print
    where I have stepped
    lies written in the sand.
    How swift the wash,
    the beating waves
    that tempt it from the land.

My body might not dare the realms
    where bluest waters sleep,
    where cold and currents,
    gallant beasts
    lie waiting in the deep.

But if the sunset's gaze I find,
    if swells at peace I see,
    a silhouette goes dancing by –
    my spirit on the sea.

Two

The moon soars in the
　　blackened canopy.
　　The starlings – fish-form
　　take the sky in waves.
　　The bubble of the hummer's
　　flashing wing
　　floods currents in my heart
　　as morning raves.

Another day to fascinate,
　　as colors flair before my eyes.

Another day with open hands,
　　to keep my ache, my joy,
　　my small reply.

Three

White sunlight glimmers on the sea,
 invoking insight, just a spark
 of worlds beyond reality,
 of voices hushed from waters dark.

There stories drift, far out of reach

so stay not safe on deck or shore,
 so cast to winds, so waters breach
 through deeps
 though peril
 find the door –
 and boldly their brave tales beseech.

Four

A ship cut loose is drifting fair –
    a shepherding gale westward glides.
    Beneath five sails like angel wings
    to glittering isles he rides.

I shout into the dancing wind
    my seaborne ecstasy.
    More wondrous though
    than his bold flight
    his sailing home shall be.

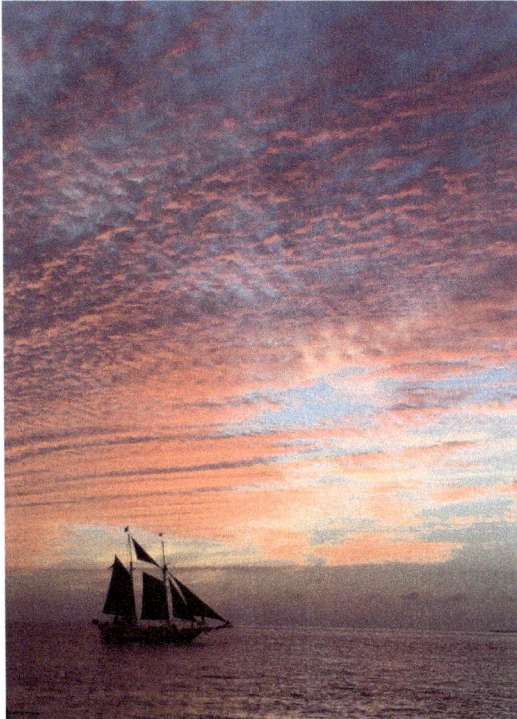

Five

Bright eyes open, I see strife
    feel pain from winds of words
    learn meanness and thinness
    from time
    watch the woods flourish
    know in my marrow
    this moment.

The gift is to be still.
    The trick is to not mind death.
    The currents of winds and waters
    roll on –
    currents carrying words
    and deluge debris,
    streams and whispers,
    hints from days gone.

Sunlight, moonlight,
    starlight reaching, bathing.

The secret lies in sensing
    one presence,
    like a great raptor alighting
    in a high rook
    and folding his wings.

Stirring winds brush my cheek –
    winds that touch everything.

Six

Mountains keep deep time inside
    their cavern halls, where tales abide –
    striated walls to hearers speak –
    bright jewels confide to them who seek
    the record of the fire and loam
    that sculpted caves to serve as home.

And sea abysses break to show
    the oldest days that Earth doth know.
    So long we, former days to claim,
    that we might understand our fame.
    But olden tales might pale before
    the days that lie on further shore.

A thousand years beyond this night –
    what name shall mark
    this coastal bight?

These pages, blank, before us stand,
    so writ by rock, so read by hand.

Seven

At the falling of day
    for a second
    I see it –
    a glimpse of the mountains
    that loom high full west.

But just clouds, it seems
    'till the golden
    light brushes
    sure slopes with an alpenglow
    cast on their peaks.

And it's only a blue sky
    that washes
    such shores
    but the blue my eye touches –
    a county high floating, unmoored.

Might I sail, might I reach it
    if dreams true
    I keep?

Might I discover
    the high coasts
    where faerie tales sleep?

Eight

If I am warm or safe or sated,
     let it be by a sustenance
     all hands can touch.

No ambrosia, but Earth's chemistry –
     sunlight and water.

Let my thanks be manifest
     to the giver
     a returning to the Earth of these goods.

This is no transactional exchange,
     but a self at rest in the arms of Earth,
     while he administers blessings.

And then the work taken up
     by my hands
     as he sleeps –
     dreams of his lands and seas
     flourishing.

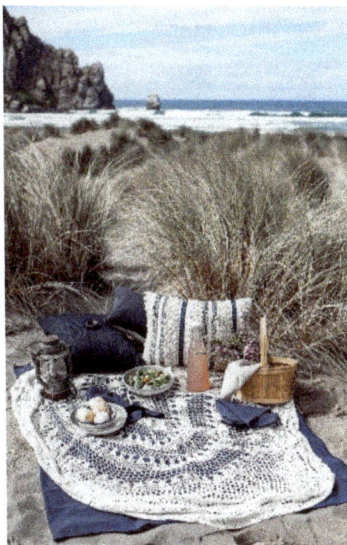

Nine

Alice had her looking glass,
    so Lucy found her wardrobe door.
    Frodo dared his mountain pass,
    and Ben Gunn kept his craft, his oar.

Crystal blue – the atmosphere
    dividing me from starry dreams –
    so set I forth into the clear
    as twilight rends my story's seams.

Ten

How lucky – every little pearl,
    their value great appraised.

At heart, a common grain of sand
    whose fortunes last are raised.

But lucky cannot be ascribed
    to one of flesh, of sight.

At core – a heart, a mind, a hand
    holds value at its height.

Eleven

Upon Earth's desolation walk we,
    stymied, lost –
    children wandering dead wastes.

And yet – there glides over stones
    water for new-languaged tongues
    and green leafed discoveries
    riddled with secrets and seeds.

Marooned on this island –
    encroaches despair.
    Yet find we the self
    not barren of tools –
    but minds sharp, but metal to harness
    the light-feeding treetops
    and storm fire blooming.

And stars –
    ingenuity visits to build crystal palaces
    for their fair light.

And so prosper we,
    upon planet's blank face,
    stowaways never, not vagrants,
    nor thieves,
    but scientists, wizards, and kings
    all are we!

Twelve

Come riptides, storm winds,
    days of pain,
    the spirit, anchored, softly speaks
    the magic words that light the dawn,
    that calm the rage, that still the sea –
    words flickering in advance of suns –
    the strongest wisdom:
    Let it be.

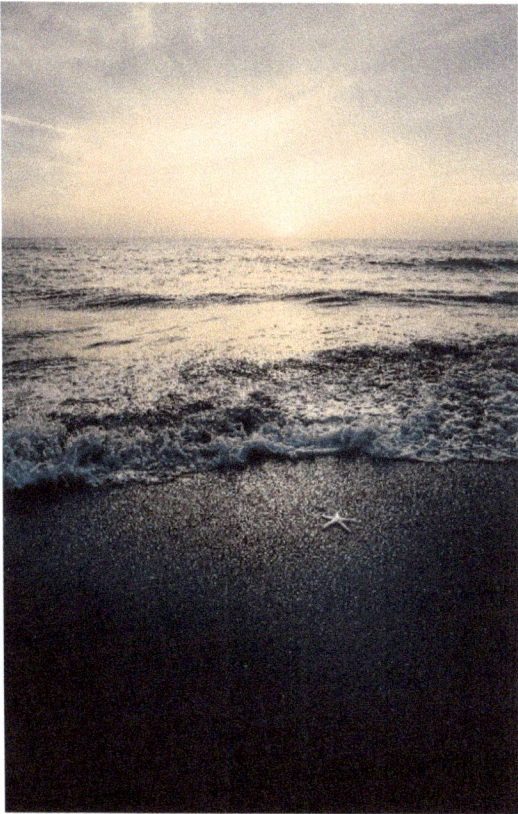

Thirteen

One loss conquers not.
  One typhoon can be weathered.
  But strike after strike after strike –
  my grieved ship haunts untethered.

Fourteen

When night falls still,
    trees cease to quake
    winds quiet be
    stars gently wake.

At such an hour
    I listen deep.
    I strain to hear
    what secrets keep
    beyond the reach
    of earthen ways
    to handsome climbs
    and firmer stays.

Yet though I hark
    in quiet bounds,
    no still small voice
    beside me sounds.

A voice in mind, though,
    softly teaches.

So I find
    the holy reaches.

Fifteen

Pleasure comes in mists not seen
  until delightful waves kiss skin.

A peering forward, looking back,
  phantasm happiness shafts in.

Sixteen

Made was heart for lover's hands –
    left lone it sweeps as desert sands.

Relief runs scarce, the waters deep
    low in the Earth, in time's slow keep.

But patient living moments each
    for their own sake hearts finally reach

the shore where winds rise into waves
    and bear the heart to love's embrace.

Seventeen

May my love take his rest
    upon my smooth-stoned shore
    and from my cup of palm to drink
    to tend what aches ring sore.

Though torrents tear the coast
    and blow
    the strong sailed boats to ocean's base
    though heavens fall and waters storm
    and raise the mists that hide the face –

my love has reasons none to quake.
    For present in my cove so still,
    together seek we deeper springs
    that light of presence e'er shall fill.

Eighteen

From shore, the sea is vast –
    before my eyes, the ocean turns
    from silver loving blue
    to gold, to gray, to black at last.

The waves, they rock, they draw,
    each crest and trough,
    a hand outstretched,
    each coiling roll caressing skin
    a word of love, a call.

Nineteen

The future all alluring.
    The past sweet in its pain.
    This present day enduring.
    I cannot pin you, peace to gain.

Why come you not with handles,
    or in a basket gathered?
    Present day, romance me not
    for to your hands I'm tethered.

So soft you slip as waters
    so take I oar and sail
    and be I focused so embarked
    that I might glimpse your shining tail.

Twenty

Gentle rains – come back to me
   the Earth to cool, the sea to sate
   let drops of sky caress the pine
   and on its needles meditate.

Soot storms rage – I see your pain
   the illness churning wild your reach
   to lash your shores and feed your fires
   no strength our willful minds to teach.

But might we yet be teacher same
   and healer keen to read your pain,
   to diagnose our greed and waste –
   let peace make soft your troubled rain.

Twenty-One

The sea begins his romance
    laying kisses at my feet
    then falls back treading
    water blue, his silver eyes on me.

I sit on mirrored sands
    while he shows off
    his competence,
    his handling the wind.

I coy turn my gaze away –
    a lover's invitation
    and he knows
    my heart so rushes wild
    so cradles he the skin
    of my bare feet,
    my thighs –
    my belly reached
    his chill relieves all heat.

No choice have I but to immerse,
    to find the strike of cool
    deep in the core
    each frigid wave –
    and I am bitten.
    Still.
    Resigned to let him
    carry me away.

Twenty-Two

From nearing roads
    at sight of ocean swells
    in pieces crumble I
    for heart of mine
    no more can hold such blue
    such seagull's cry
    and onto shore I crash
    and run to breathless meet
    a wisest friend –

this ancient thrashing sea.

Twenty-Three

The colors of the west
    upon the sea
    such beauty
    little stars feel called
    and can't resist
    to with them shine

so dawns the night.

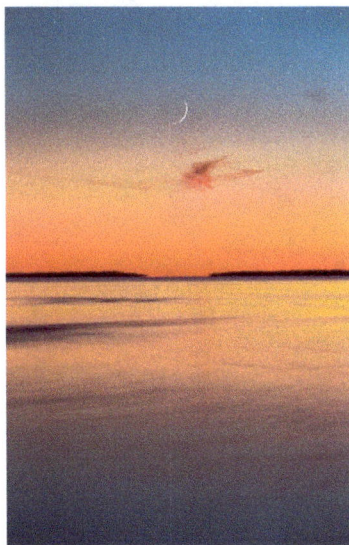

Twenty-Four

Fluid moves the river
    through the trees –
    sky river blue or black or white
    and carrying loads of faerie dust –
    of seeds and spore flown as a kite.

And galleon ships of clouds cruise by
    on highest reach of winding winds
    so watch and cling to holdfast tree
    while Earth keels aft and bends.

Twenty-Five

A water world
    sapphiric spins
    in space.

One satellite
    to summon waves
    in dance.

One sun
    to storm clouds wake
    and spill.

A chemistry
    to call forth
    living plants.

Twenty-Six

The birds have swooped
    from twilit nests
    and gathered on the mossy eaves.

The golden glow of risen moon
    seems what they've come to see.

Shy, he slips from tangled limbs –
    coy, he catches every eye –
    aglow, his cheeks betray his gaze
    upon the vanished sun yet nigh.

Soft – a candle – is his shimmer
    soothed, the birds he sets to sleep
    yet draws he strong the tide of oceans
    drives he wild the currents deep.

Twenty-Seven

The solar disc Elysian slips
    into the day –
    a red balloon

and drifting through the skies sapphiric
    up to heights –
    a Phoenix gold

and meeting finally western countries,
    painting seas –
    a prism winging.

Twenty-Eight

Sail not away, brilliant sun of the west
    for without you the darkness
    will spread
    and will blight out the trees
    and will drain gray the grass
    and will nettle my spirit with dread.

Sail you must? Take me with you
    I bet I could fly if you lend me
    a feathering of wings
    and your white southern wind
    and your spirit ablaze –
    I shall dash in your wake,
    bold and free.

But you've left. Now the night.
    And the birds in retreat flicker black
    but – a starfield of candles
    you've lit by the dozens
    you've set in the windows –
    a promise that you will sail back.

Twenty-Nine

Far strange how medium of ocean
    works upon a human soul
    in ways that landforms cannot touch –
    a magic cast by pitch and roll.

A blue to match the atmosphere
    a black to mirror galaxy
    a deep where beastlings
    maintain sway
    in waves that dance a ship to sea.

Thirty

What harm be borne by
    the ending of worlds?

Say the sun crashes west
    say the blue solstice shades
    say the hand wears a fault
    say the Earth takes what's hers.

Does the Earth not flush green
    do not faults signal stories
    won't evenshine linger
    the western sun merry?

The finale is gentle –
    a rising of stars.

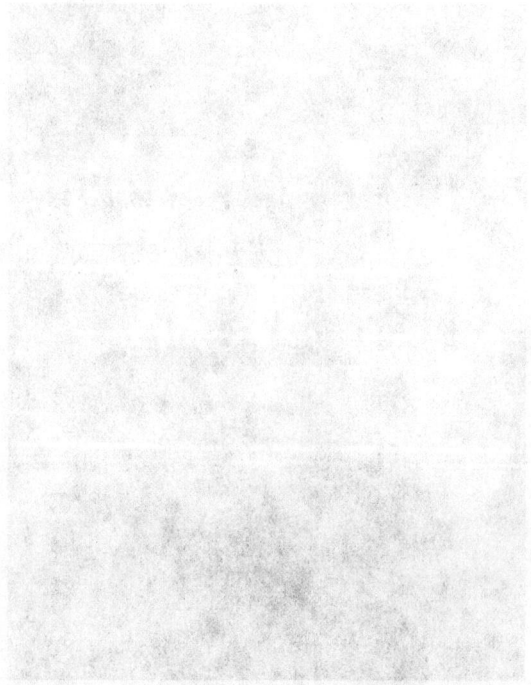

Photography Contributed By

1. Louis Hansel
2. Philip Graves
3. James Donovan
4. Jim Davis
5. Chris Sabor
6. Mike Setchell
7. Laura Vinck Hyu
8. Sixteen Miles Out
9. Viktor Vasicsek
10. Andre Alexander
11. Vincent Ledvina
12. Todd Trapani
13. Zoltan Tasi
14. Bowen Chin
15. Monica Gozalo
16. Sarah Granger
17. Sofia Ornelas
18. Jezael Malgoza
19. Phoebe Dill
20. Diana Roberts
21. Jeremy Bishop
22. Mateus Araujo
23. Lianhao Qu
24. Jasper Graetsch
25. James Coleman
26. Federico Di Dio
27. Casey Horner
28. Casey Horner
29. Johannes Plenio
30. Even Leith

Free eBook

NIGHT SWIFTLY FALLING
BY TRICIA D. WAGNER

EIGHT-YEAR-OLD SWIFT IS LOST IN DREAMS OF SEA LEGENDS
AND PIRATE ADVENTURES, UNTIL AN ENCOUNTER WITH THE
DEADLY POWER OF THE OCEAN SHOCKS HIM INTO REALITY.
SWIFT STRUGGLES TO HANG ONTO HIS CHILDHOOD FANTASIES,
BUT HIS NEW UNDERSTANDING OF THE FRAGILE NATURE OF
LIFE AND FRIENDSHIPS THREATENS TO SWAMP HIS HOPE.
UNDER THE GUIDANCE OF HIS OLDER BROTHER, CAIUS,
SWIFT MUST LEARN TO BRAVE THE CHALLENGING WAVES OF
CHANGE WITHOUT LOSING HIMSELF TO THEIR DESTRUCTION.

Also by Tricia D. Wagner

SWIFT & THE STAR OF ATLANTIS SERIES

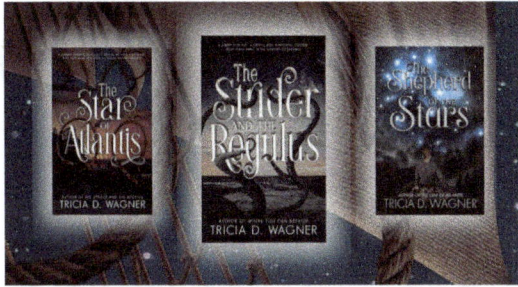

A STARRY-EYED BOY. A CRYPTIC MAP. A MYTHICAL TREASURE. WHAT PERILS AWAIT IN THE CHASING OF DREAMS?

As Swift lives up to his name and his family legacy, young adults receive a fast-paced fantasy that will appeal not just on the adventure or fantasy levels, but in matters of the heart as the young struggle for independence and action in the face of parental restrictions. Tricia D. Wagner's attention to pairing psychological struggle with the adventure of finding a promised treasure creates a story that pulls on the emotions of young readers as it satisfies their desire for action and adventure.

-D. Donovan, Senior Reviewer, Midwest Book Review

Also by Tricia D. Wagner

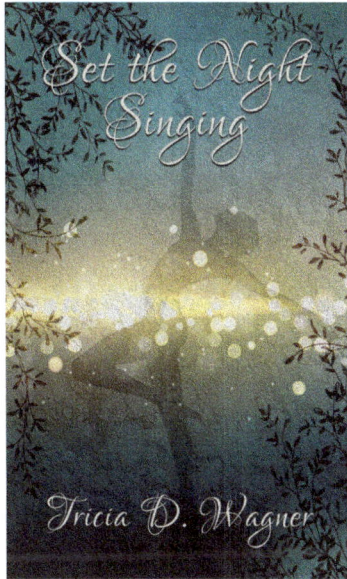

SET THE NIGHT SINGING

WE ARE IN DESPERATE NEED OF THE PHYSICAL WORLD, THE SENSUOUS, THE SMALLEST TEXTURE, A REMINDER THAT WE ARE MORTAL. ONLY THEN WILL WE REMEMBER TO CARE.

TRICIA D. WAGNER IS YOUR ANSWER. IN THESE POEMS YOU'LL FIND BALM, YOUR HOPE FOR FINDING HOPE. -NINA SCHUYLER, AUTHOR OF THE TRANSLATOR

Also by Tricia D. Wagner

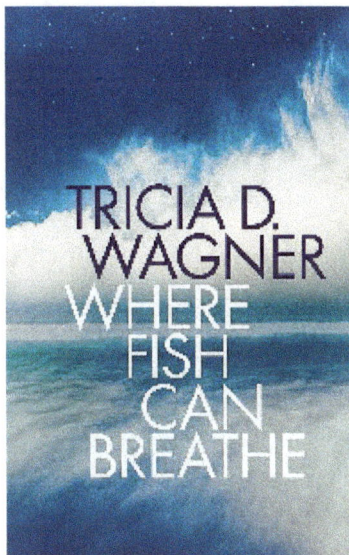

Where Fish Can Breathe

Ten-year-old Swift longs to be as grown up as his brothers, but confronting himself in the wilds of the North Atlantic, he must contend with what it means to be a man.

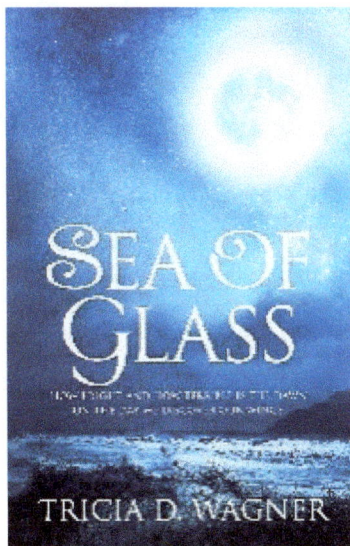

SEA OF GLASS

WHEN AN OLD ANGLER PRESSES TEO TO SEEK A GODDESS—THE SEA ANGEL—FOR RESCUE, TEO SETS OUT ALONG BAJA'S WILD COAST TO TEST WHETHER HELP CAN BE FOUND AT THE HANDS OF THE GODS.

TO LEARN THE TRUTH, HE MUST LOOK BEYOND LEGENDS AND SUMMON THE COURAGE TO CHALLENGE HIS PAPÁ.

AND TO REACH FREEDOM, HE MUST TAP HIS OWN STRENGTH, HIDDEN BENEATH WOUNDS LAID BY GLASS.

Also by Tricia D. Wagner

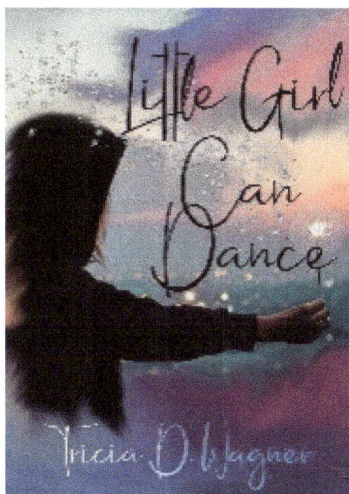

LITTLE GIRL CAN DANCE

A DANCER. A CREATURE. A SPIRE-CAPPED AND LONELY BOARDING SCHOOL.

LITTLE GIRL CAN DANCE IS A SPELLBINDING TALE TOLD OVER SIX SWEEPING ACTS. TRICIA D. WAGNER'S SIGNATURE STYLE IS ON TOP FORM IN THIS BEAUTIFUL NOVELLA.

A WONDERFUL FUSION OF POETIC PROSE AND LIMITLESS IMAGINATION PLUNGES YOU STRAIGHT INTO ANDROMEDA'S MESMERISING WORLD.

PREPARE TO HAVE YOUR HEART BROKEN AND MENDED AGAIN IN THIS SHORT BUT STUNNING FABLE.

-ELEANOR HAWKEN, AUTHOR OF THE BLUE LADY AND SAMMY FERAL'S DIARIES OF WEIRD

About the Author

TRICIA D. WAGNER IS AN AWARD-WINNING NOVELIST, POET, AND SHORT STORY WRITER. SHE GREW UP IN AMARILLO, TEXAS, CHASING STORMS, RIDING STALLIONS, SOJOURNING THROUGH PAINTED CANYONS, DISAPPEARING INTO FLOATING MESAS UNDER STARRY SKIES.

SHE NOW LIVES IN ROCKFORD, ILLINOIS (THOUGH THE TRUTH IS, SHE'S A CITIZEN OF A DOZEN FICTIONAL COUNTRIES.) TRICIA WORKS IN EDUCATION AND LIVES DAY TO DAY WONDERSTRUCK BUT LUCKILY CAN FEEL HER WAY ABOUT THIS TERRIFYING, BEAUTIFUL EARTH THROUGH WRITING.

TRICIA HAS PIECES PUBLISHED IN THE *WRITE CITY MAGAZINE*, *CHICAGO NEWA*, *WORD OF ART 3D*, *LITERARY YARD*, AND *MIDWEST REVIEW*.

Author's Note

I LOVE CONNECTING WITH READERS AND WRITERS. IF, YOU'RE INTERESTED IN STORIES, THEN YOU'RE A KINDRED SPIRIT TO ME, AND I HAVE LOTS MORE IN STORE FOR YOU.

TO QUOTE ANOTHER KINDRED SPIRIT IN WRITING, JEDI MASTER STEPHEN KING:

"WRITING IS MAGIC, AS MUCH AS THE WATER OF LIFE AS ANY OTHER ART. THE WATER IS FREE. SO DRINK. DRINK AND BE FILLED UP."

IF YOU'RE INTERESTED NOT ONLY IN STORIES, BUT IN STORY CREATION, VISIT MY WEBSITE AND SIGN UP TO RECEIVE A FREE **STORY KICKOFF CHARACTER WORKSHEET.**

I DESIGNED THIS TOOL FOR THAT FIRST MOMENT OF GETTING OUR FEET WET AT THE BRINK OF A STORY.

TO GET YOUR FREE WORKSHEET, VISIT:
www.TriciaWagner.com

www.ingramcontent.com/pod-product-compliance
Lightning Source LLC
Chambersburg PA
CBHW070028030426
42335CB00017B/2342